D1565763

Dear Lady Debra,
    Thank you for showing up
in my life and making it so much better!

                        Love you Always!

the
blessing
point

An Immigration Story of
Love and Liberty in God

Naseem Matteson

Copyright © 2019 Naseem Matteson.

All rights reserved. This book or any portion thereof may not be reproduced or used in any manner whatsoever without the express written permission of the publisher except for the use of brief quotations in a book review.

FIRST EDITION

Designed by Brandy Sappington

www.smallbusinessabcs.com

ISBN 9781698806778

Dedicated to Professor Syed Karaar Husain,
St. Patrick's Government College

To the first Christian man in my life who spoke to my
future as a young businesswoman in USA before there
was any sign of it in my life. May he rest in peace.

TABLE OF CONTENTS

ACKNOWLEDGEMENTS

I will praise thee, O Lord, with my whole heart;
I will shew forth all thy marvelous works.

PSALM 9:1

I simply must thank the who people inspired me in so many ways, either through encouraging words, their acts of kindness, and their positivity towards my existence.

To my family Patricia Ruth Dearing, Craig Matteson, Shamim Ahmed, Ghayas Ahmed and Gramma Bea Woodland.

To my friends from Wade's Super Market Mary Lee, Kathy Bishop, Connie Marshal, Tony (R.I.P) & Deborah Sedinger.

To my first client Debra Dear, thank you for taking a chance on me!

To my Naval family Amber Waller, Melissa Phelps, Paul Jensen, James Maupin, Timothy French, Michael Smith, John Kearney, Nadine Glazka, and Ashley Wessling.

And of course, I have to thank my sweet husband Curtis Matteson and my amazing boys. You fill my life with abundant joy every day.

Thank you to every person who played a role (whether knowing or unknowing) in helping me get where I am today.

INTRODUCTION

Thy word is a lamp unto my feet,
and a light unto my path.

PSALM 119:105

As a young girl living in Pakistan, I never would have dreamed that I could grow up to become a United States citizen. It would have seemed even more far-fetched to think that I would go on to serve in the U.S. Navy and then become a successful online business owner.

The political climate of my home country was so unstable, that all that was expected of Pakistani girls was to finish high school, marry into a decent family and maybe (if you're lucky) become a school teacher. And even those opportunities were riddled with prejudice and conspiracy.

But thinking back, I can start to trace the beautiful thread of my life through my relationship with Christ. He was present for every single struggle, every single obstacle but his touch is also on every single win and accomplishment I have made.

As I look at the political climate and tension in the U.S. surrounding immigration, I am saddened by the ignorance and contempt displayed on both sides of the argument. I know what it feels like to desperately want to start a new life yet feel trapped in a situation you can't control.

After experiencing the grueling legal immigration process first-hand, I understand how some people could be tempted to try to bypass the obstacles entirely. As an immigrant, I feel it's my duty to share my experience in hopes of inspiring you to stay the course and trust that the Lord will deliver you from the despair.

In the coming chapters I will share my journey and the lessons I learned as a Christian woman immigrating to America from a war-torn Pakistan. I can only hope that my story will empower you to take a chance on building your dream, to hold steadfast to your faith in Christ along the way and to encourage patience and compassion from people both sides of the experience.

May our Lord bless you and keep you.

PART ONE

DISCIPLINE

1

Family First

Children, obey your parents in all things:
for this is well pleasing unto the Lord.

COLOSSIANS 3:20

Everyone automatically assumes that because I immigrated to the U.S., that I must have been fleeing for my life or fleeing from inhumane treatment in my third world, home country.

The truth is, that while things were incredibly hard for my family living in Pakistan (which I'll get into a bit more later in the book), it isn't what you likely pictured it to be. You would be shocked to learn that we probably have so many similarities between our lives, things that you have never even considered. Yet I still made what seems to many, an impossible decision to journey across the ocean and start a new life.

Honestly, that fact itself is one of the very reasons I was so moved to share my story with the world. There are so many preconceived notions and misconceptions about what motivates a person or family to uproot their lives and move to a foreign land.

Yes, the numbers of people who make this choice under duress probably far outweigh those who didn't, and I would never make light of anyone's suffering.

However, some people merely want something more than what's available to them, even if "what they have" isn't what some people would consider "unbearable." In fact, I have many good memories of my early childhood.

You see, I get my spirit from my mother. Although she seemed meek and mild, in some of the day to day handling of household things, she was fierce and independent in her thinking; she was progressive compared to most, especially for those days in Pakistan.

For instance, my parents had a marriage of love, as opposed to a traditional arranged marriage. Even as a young woman, she took a stand against her family and stood up for her belief that marriage should be made in love. This was something that she instilled in all of her children.

As you read through my story, look for those sparks that she passed on to each of her children. The truth is we all have the power to change traditions and live life as we dream, instead of what others desire for us.

FOR I KNOW THE PLANS I HAVE FOR YOU

As a family, we traveled a lot. My father worked for the Saudi airline as a ground equipment officer and we would go back and forth between Pakistan to Saudi Arabia several times a year. This was normal for us. And thanks to having four siblings, I never had to worry about making new friends. I had natural born friends, who traveled with me wherever I went.

My mother, who was once a teacher, homeschooled us while we were in Saudi Arabia. My older sisters stayed back in Pakistan with my grandmother because the language was Arabic in Saudi Arabia and my brothers and I stayed with my parents in Arabia.

Unfortunately, my dad had to leave his job after a few years. Although he was excellent at it, he was not a Saudi citizen (a requirement for maintaining employment in the country long term). The airline gave him an ultimatum: he could train two people to take over his job and he could return to Pakistan or they would give him an American visa so he could start a life there instead.

My father made the difficult choice to go to America. It was a long process, so, while he waited for the visa, he trained the replacement workers and we all eventually joined my sisters back in Pakistan.

At that time, we had no idea that we would all be coming to America. The plan was for my dad to go there, work and save up money, then return home to us in Pakistan. Nobody told us that we would one day be asked to travel to an unknown land.

My parents bought a nice apartment in a gated community and the five of us joined a real school. For the first time, we were all together and enjoying a stable life of going to school and enjoying life all together with both parents.

My mom always valued education. She wanted us to go to college, find jobs, become independent and then if we found someone that we love, pursue them. Most girls in Pakistan were only expected to marry and or become a school teacher. I'm so grateful that my mother wanted more for me and my sisters.

My dad on the other hand, was more old-fashioned and leaned towards his family's rules and traditions. Like any child, he wanted to please his parents. You can imagine how upset he was when my mother decided to put me in a co-ed school to help out my brother with his studies.

He was having a difficult time, keeping up with homework and listening in class. That was a big deal to BOTH sides of the family, because traditionally boys go to "boy" school and girls go to "girl" school.

Even though I was his little sister, I helped him stay on task, sat with him and explained his homework. Eventually, I was helping all of my brothers' friends with their homework too. To be honest, I really enjoyed tutoring him all the way through to graduation.

For some children, skipping a grade would be traumatic. It's funny looking back because I don't think I knew early on that I wasn't like "most" children. Discipline in all things was just my normal.

As I got older, I became more ambitious, by digging into the things I excelled in. I enjoyed learning and knew I could have a great life if I worked for it.

HONOR YOUR FATHER AND YOUR MOTHER

Have you ever thought about how significant authority and discipline are in your life? It literally bleeds over into every single aspect. It impacts your jobs and professional relationships, your health and fitness, your personal relationships, your education, how we parent, how we serve customers in our businesses… the list goes on and on. That being said, there has to be a balance with fun as well.

As much as we were disciplined, we also pulled our fair share of shenanigans. I remember once when we were younger, my siblings and I wanted a puppy so badly. But 20-30 years ago, in Pakistan, people didn't think dogs were suitable indoor pets. Many Muslims believed dogs are filthy and should only be permitted outside as guard dogs, never to be allowed in the house.

My sister decided to sneak two adorable puppies in the house and keep them in our bedroom. And that week, we had the time of our lives! We worked together and took care of them, kept them quiet and played with them. It was a week before our puppies were discovered and boy were, we in trouble!

My dad got so upset that he gave the family an ultimatum: we had to choose between him and the dog staying. (His plans had a way of backfiring.) Like some bold band of rebel soldiers, all five of us stood up and declared we chose our dogs.

We didn't care what the cost was, we just loved our dogs. We were so incredibly strong willed. How insane is it to think we would actually choose our dogs over our father?

Of course, we wouldn't, but in that moment (and many others that followed) we understood the importance of standing with each other in an effort to protect our dream; to protect our newest furry family members.

Sadly, we had to get rid of one right away and my brothers friend said he would take him to a farm and give him a good life. We did get to keep the other dog and named him Tiger. He was the only dog that we have ever owned. I walked him every single morning before school, and any extra time I could.

Even when things were tough, Tiger was so smart, and sensitive to our situation. At one point when my family lost everything (more on that later), my parents tried as hard as they could to protect us from the stress. But we noticed. We noticed that when we got home from school, there was no food on the table. We noticed that mom had to beg our family members to help us out.

Yet, when we would come home from school and see nothing on the table for dinner, that dog would find his bones hidden in shoes, or under the couch and set them before us as if to share. Tiger often left us speechless. That dog was such a blessing in our lives.

As I've grown, I've learned to look for those tiny signs that God is watching out for me, even in the most difficult times.

THROUGH THE PRAISE OF CHILDREN

As a child I absolutely LOVED cricket and I would play with all of the older kids. My dad would just shake his head and say, "This girl is going to have us running around…I can't believe she plays cricket." I'm so grateful our parents encouraged us to explore and make some choices for ourselves.

The average girl growing up in Pakistan heard a lot of the word "shouldn't". Girls shouldn't play with boys, girls shouldn't wear jeans, girls shouldn't attend school with boys. However, if we wanted to wear jeans, then we did. If I wanted to go outside and hang out with my brothers' friends, then I would.

I also loved making things. My mother used to tell me that I was my dad's favorite because I brewed the best tea in the world. My dad even liked to brag about it. When his friends would come over to visit, I always got to be the one to make them tea. I was so proud.

As a parent I strive to encourage my children where they struggle and praise them for the things they excel at. Everything we do has a ripple effect that will last for generations beyond me. I'm grateful that I grew up in such a supportive home.

Even at a young age, I learned that it was in my nature to nurture others. I loved cleaning the house because it helped my parents. I would do anything and everything new and exciting. I wanted to live life to the fullest and have the kind of happy-go-lucky attitude that spreads joy to others.

I used to get up at 6:00 in the morning, enjoy my tea and walk the dog outside. I would make breakfast, have it all set out and ready and then wake my brothers and sisters up for school. My parents did their own thing and I nurtured my siblings.

I love being able to reflect back on some of those more innocent times. As a mother myself, I can't help but laugh about some of our shenanigans but also be grateful to my parents for the things that they instilled in us. I honestly believe they laid a strong foundation for us growing up.

Even though our lives got so difficult from time to time, their example gave us security. We knew that as long as we kept our eyes on Christ, strived for excellence in all we did and remained focused and grateful, there was nothing we couldn't overcome.

ACTION STEP: *LOVE*

I ACCEPT MY FAMILY JUST AS THEY ARE

List some of the ways you may appear
judgmental or critical to your family.

_____

_____

_____

_____

_____

_____

_____

_____

_____

_____

_____

Sometimes, you may not agree with the actions of loved
ones. However, judgment should be left to God. He
loves us in spite of our flaws and our disobedience. We
should love and support each other just as fiercely.

2

An Eager Student

How much better is it to get wisdom than gold! and to get understanding rather to be chosen than silver!

PROVERBS 16:16

After I graduated high school, it was time for me to decide what it was I wanted to do with my life. I knew that I loved nurturing my family and was very interested in becoming a homeopathic doctor in Pakistan.

So, once I was done with school, I drove out to the homeopathic school. It was an hour and a half away from our house both to and from. To attend there, I was going to have to take public transportation and switch buses twice.

My mother was not okay with her little girl traveling that far on a public bus and she told me, "You have to think about something else." Since I loved numbers, I decided to pursue accounting.

I knew St. Patrick's Government College had the best program for commerce, but it was very difficult to be accepted. So, I was excited and nervous to meet the college Dean and see if he would accept me into his program.

On the day of my interview I was quite shocked at the way the Dean presented himself. Usually, college Deans look very professional; they wear suits and have neat hair. But THIS Dean looked like a Pakistani Hippy.

He had long hair and because of his polio, he always wore a special boot on his foot. He only spoke English, and had a reputation of asking prospective students the same starting question: "Do you know how to speak English?" If you did, you passed onto the next level and if not... well he would ask you to leave the building.

Thankfully, I managed to speak English with him. When he asked me why I liked accounting I answered, "Because debt and credit are all the same in any country. It is international. I am really interested in it and I want to be a chartered accountant." He accepted my application and I joined St. Patrick's Government College.

WHOSO LOVETH INSTRUCTION LOVETH KNOWLEDGE

It was the best time of my life. That teacher was the very best one that I have ever had. He made me feel like I was going on to do bigger and better things in life, and that my family's circumstances were not the end of the world.

He saw greatness in me…. way before I ever did. It's an incredible thing to have someone see something special in you and really believe you are capable of greatness. There is so much power in encouraging and speaking positivity into another person.

There were 120 students in the class and SOMEHOW, he would point to me every time he had an example that he wanted the class to learn.

"Naseem is starting a business and she started selling office supplies…."

Or

"Naseem went to America and opened a business…."

Every time he started to look for an example, I would look at him and think "Oh no…he's gonna…" and sure enough, he always did.

I was embarrassed and worried that everyone would make fun of me because of his extra attention. Every time he would talk about me, I would blush. But I was proud too.

It's true what they say that we are the sum of the 5 people closest to us. When you surround yourself with people who not only lift you up but who are on a path of success, you begin to see opportunity you would have otherwise overlooked. Your mindset begins to shift. You become brave and bold. You are better able to pivot around obstacles that stand between you and your goals.

A WICKED RULER OVER A POOR PEOPLE

While I was still in college, my sister held her four-year degree and began to try her best to find work. But sadly, in Pakistan 30 years ago, it was a man's world and everywhere she went to apply for work, instead of asking about her knowledge and know how they would instead ask her why she wasn't married and that she shouldn't even look for work. That she should get married like a good Pakistan woman and not worry about money.

Soon more and more people started questioning us on our education and choices for our own life and they found out that our father had gone to America. They looked down on us even more and thought that our father abandoned us. Nobody liked the choices that our father made, and they told us as often as they could.

By the time I was done with my third year of college, my father had received his American citizenship. He had been in the U.S for four years and my mother decided that we all needed to be with him. That only in America could we all make something of our lives.

She was desperate to give us all the best chance that she could and adamant that we could not find it in Pakistan, where the corrupt rules of money and bribery were more important than good grades and family values.

My mother told my dad that we will save even more money and get even more jobs, anything it takes to get her children to a place where they can choose the life they want to lead. She felt that one of us would get killed if we stayed, between the politics and the bribery.

30 years ago, Pakistan was a very different country than it is today. When I was growing up it was a corrupt country for the rich. If you had money you could go to the college they wanted, but for the poor or the middle class, you had to bribe people to get the things that you wanted or needed.

If you wanted a good job, out of a speeding ticket or a telephone line in your house, you had to bribe to get it.

If you wanted any chance at all of a high paying job or to be in the military, you had to bribe to get in. And of course, we were middle class, and had nothing to bribe with.

My older sister decided that she wanted to be a doctor, but because we didn't have money, she couldn't go to the schools that she needed to receive a medical education.

My other sister wanted to become an architect, and even with saving to go to America, my parents struggled even more so she could go to this architectural school. This school was not easy to get in and she achieved it.

Sadly, after achieving all A's in her classes, a rich family bought her transcript through the bribing system. This disheartened my sister and she realized that it didn't matter how good your grades were if you didn't have the money to back them up.

I thought, why can't we all just be happy, do the right thing and enjoy life? Everybody has rights, People were just trying to work hard to become someone or to do something. Why was this such a challenge for others to see? Why is it always such a challenge for others to just let people be happy?

If they don't want to be Muslim, they shouldn't have too.

If they don't want to work to support their family, they shouldn't have too.

If they don't want to get married, they should be able to do this without people butting into their business.

My older brother was getting caught up in political arguments. In Pakistan, you either choose your party or they will come to your house and take anything that they want. He started to feel the pressure and it affected his college education.

Everything felt unsafe. And it seemed like everyone from extended family to our government was out to hurt us as a family. We did our best to concentrate on our education and ignore our family who always had something to say about our lives, or the choices that our parents made.

They felt that our father didn't know what he was doing and that us girls should just get married because that is what all good Pakistan girls did. And good Pakistan boys got married and moved their parents and his whole family in to one big ole house to take care of everyone.

But thankfully, our mother was adamant that we be independent. That is what she was fighting so hard for. She even hired all five of us a teacher so we could learn how to drive. We learned on a stick shift because that was the most relevant for vehicles back there. Everyone looked down on her even more for that.

I know that currently, Pakistan is a totally different world. Women are working, they are even pilots and, in the military, if they choose. But growing up in that country and dealing with women being treated so differently, made a huge impact on us.

While women were expected to become teachers, nurses or work in the banks, I chose accounting because I can do it anywhere. I chose to be different because my mother always encouraged her girls to work in whatever field we wanted too. It's one of the most precious gifts she ever gave us.

ACTION STEP: *STUDY*

EDUCATION IS MY PATH TO FREEDOM

List some of the ways money can have a positive
impact on you and the lives around you.

_____

_____

_____

_____

_____

_____

_____

_____

_____

_____

_____

It's okay not to know everything. Commit to try to
improve yourself every day. Wisdom is developed
through experience and discerning study.

3

Count Your Blessings... And Your Cash

For which of you, intending to build a tower, sitteth not down first, and counteth the cost, whether he have sufficient to finish it?

LUKE 14:28

As you can see by now, my childhood wasn't all rainbows and roses. Every story has a villain. In my story, one villain was introduced by a knock on the door.

BEWARE OF FALSE PROPHETS

You see, my father was extremely unhappy living in Pakistan. He worked a lot and did his own thing while my mother oversaw our education. My dad wanted MORE from life and was unsure how to do that with such an unstable political climate.

I've seen it so many times in my life. People want so badly to catch that "big break" so they are more susceptible to being taken advantage of. So, when an investor approached my dad and offered him a quick solution for getting more out of life, it's no wonder he blindly accepted.

My father was offered an 'opportunity' to invest in an idea and was told that if he did, he would make SO much money that he would never have to work again. It was a 'word of mouth' agreement, which means there were no legal agreements, and no papers signed. Even as a child I felt in my gut that it was a bad idea.

However, he believed the dream he was sold; that he could invest a little bit of money, grow it into recurring income and live happily ever after. My parents decided to go ahead and invest, sold our apartment and put all of their savings from working for seven years, into the deal.

And it left us with nothing.

You know what they say, "If it walks like a duck and quacks like a duck…it's not a million dollars…. IT'S A DUCK!"

With nothing, my dad had to literally wake up and smell the coffee. He had five children in school, had zero income and almost no savings. Hitting rock bottom not only is humbling, but it's lonely.

See, before my dad got swindled, our parents had been fairly well off. All of our family and friends were happy; they came around, they showed up. But when we lost all of our money, we started to see people for who they truly were. Not only did we lose our money and our home, one by one we lost our relatives and our friends, too.

This was a very crucial time in our lives. After my dad lost all of our money, my family had to move to another town. My dad's friend was a contractor and he was building apartments. He got us in the very last one that was not sold, and he let us use it for free.

CAST BUT A GLANCE AT RICHES AND THEY ARE GONE

Soon after my dad's poor investment choices, my father's visa finally came through and he left to go to America, where he knew he could put his equipment officer education to work. He needed to be somewhere that he could support his family and be rewarded for his hard work.

My dad hoped this would turn everything around. So, we all chipped in money and sold our furniture so that he could afford his plane ticket to America. We were suddenly all *alone*.

It was a scary time. We didn't know if we would ever be able to join him. Our job was to keep our eyes on success and achieving a college degree, because whether at home in Pakistan or with my dad in America, we were determined to make it.

My mom had no idea where my dad was working or how many jobs that he had, she only had to ask him for money, and he would give it to her.

My father was working hard on saving money for this but was told that it would take a couple of years at least, for my brothers and sisters. One month, my dad forgot to send us money and we had to figure out how to survive on practically nothing.

It was then I started to help my mom manage our money. I learned early on how to budget money and how hard it is to run a household, especially when my father could not help. The one thing that got us through the hard times was our faith. We believed in God. We believed that there is a bigger power in the universe who created this world.

True, we weren't religious fanatics, but we had our belief that with God's help we were going to get out of this hole. And that even without money, as long as we had our faith, we would get through this and certainly anything that comes our way.

At a young age I had to learn to be very watchful and thoughtful. I became involved in making financial decisions on my moms' behalf because she had never had to before. My father always dealt with the money while my mother raised us kids.

As time passed, we learned so many different lessons that make up who we are in life. We learned not to depend on others to give us a hand up. We learned we were responsible to for our own happiness. And we learned to lean into our faith that God would see us through.

Proverbs 3:4-6 tells us, "Trust in the Lord with all thine heart; and lean not unto thine own understanding. In all thy ways acknowledge him, and he shall direct thy paths."

And at times that was very difficult to do, especially working on such extremely limited resources. However, we were determined to make our lives better. Every sacrifice would be worth it in the end.

ACTION STEP: *SAVE*

MONEY EXPANDS MY LIFE'S OPPORTUNITIES AND EXPERIENCES.

List some of the ways money can have a positive impact on you and the lives around you.

_____

_____

_____

_____

_____

_____

_____

_____

_____

_____

Always try to live within your means and stray from acquiring new debt. Our God wants us to live in abundance. To do that you have to save, spend and invest wisely. Make sure every penny has purpose.

PART TWO
GRIT

4

Facing Rejection

Pray without ceasing.
In everything give thanks: for this is the will of God
in Christ Jesus concerning you.

1 THESSALONIANS 5:17-18

Our family's journey to America was long and grueling. We were told it would take a few years for my brother and sisters to be able to travel to America, so we were instructed to wait for their names to come up. Once they did, we would receive a letter from America with an interview date and time.

We were all so excited about our future, but my dad felt bad that he couldn't bring everyone together at once. With the attorney fees, the airline tickets and other expenses, the trip would cost us close to $10,000. As a result, my dad stopped sending us money to live on, so he could continue to save up for Visa Fee's.

Finally, in '93 my brother and sister got "the" letter from America. We had been so worried it wouldn't come; with the corruption in the government jobs, you often could not get your mail unless you bribed a watch guard to bring it to you. Mail often turned up missing. Crooked people would just toss it away. But through God's grace that first letter came. I still remember the feeling of excitement when we all held it in our hands.

We called my father and he flew into Pakistan, gathered my siblings college degrees and important paperwork together, then took them to the American Embassy for their interview. This was the most crucial part of the process.

During the interview, you have to stand in front of the guy in charge of the American Embassy and tell them why you want to go to America, what your intentions are and what you plan to do there to make a living. If for any reason they felt like you were not telling the truth, they could reject you on the spot and you never would get another chance at a Visa.

The wait was scary, but after a successful interview both my brother and my sister were approved. While were genuinely happy they were finally going to start the next phase of their life…we were sad to see them go.

THE STEPS OF A GOOD MAN ARE ORDERED BY THE LORD

Growing up, we never needed anyone outside of our family because we always had each other to play with, grow our imaginations with and share meals with. This interview meant that our tight-knit group of "forever friends" was breaking up. My father told us that we wouldn't see each other for at least two to three years.

Our father's plan was to take them back to America where they would get their green cards, wait five years and then become citizens. He would then begin saving once more for myself and my brothers American Visas.

It was hard to stay back. And it was even harder to keep my siblings leaving a secret, but we knew we had too. To avoid further judgement or complications, we kept quiet about where my siblings went off to and kept plugging along with school while saving money.

At this point, I was going to college, my younger brother was in high school and my sister was still looking for jobs that she could succeed at with her degree.

Over in America, my brother started high school and my sister started Virginia Tech. They both had part time jobs so they could help my father pay for the rest of the family's visas.

It was so difficult to stay positive, to stay the course.

THE RIGHTEOUS CRY AND THE LORD HEARETH

Then in 1995, I spiraled into a deep depression. I was just finishing my third year in college and got denied my American Visa because I did not answer one question correctly.

I was completely heartbroken. I was also nervous to tell my parents about the denial letter. I was terrified that I would never be allowed to go to America with the rest of my family and that all of the education and wishful thinking had been for nothing.

The American Embassy told me that I would have to wait for another interview and that it could take years. As expected, my father was FURIOUS. He berated me, called me names and told me that I would never survive in this world because I did not speak up for myself.

It's funny; when things get difficult, people like to say "have faith" as if it's some magical switch you can flip to make yourself feel better or change the outcome. The reality is that faith is an action. It requires you to do more than "think" something will be better. You must actually take steps to bring it to fruition. At this point in my life, I just wasn't in a place where I could do *more*.

That was honestly the most depressing time of my life. Here I was turning 18 and felt like I would never be able to attend a US college like I had been planning. I was so depressed that I stopped talking to my friends and began losing hope in the faith I once had.

I also stopped going to college; I didn't want to finish anything. I was done. I felt that the American embassy would never give me another chance because I got rejected the first time. What had been the point of all of our hard work and frugal living?

My mom was so worried that I had lost my mind from the rejection. I even called my sister in the United States and told her "Don't worry about me. I am done. I am never ever going to America, but I need to get out of this country. I will go to college somewhere else."

I promised myself I'd get out of Pakistan by ANY means and moved forward making a plan B. I began calling people and researching other countries to see what their requirements were to get a Visa.

In my research, I decided that Australia was where my life would have to be. I would simply apply with the Australian embassy and one way or another, get out of this country!

I constantly read newspapers and job boards, and even considered joining the Australian military, just to get away.

Then, one day while going through the newspapers, I came across the obituary one of the people who believed in me the most. He had been very sick with polio. He had no children and wasn't married.

He was so independent and determined to teach through his illness. His death depressed me even more. Why should I consider going back to school here, if my favorite teacher was no longer alive to teach me?

I knew that at this point in my life, I had done everything right. I was a good sister and well-behaved daughter. I excelled in college. I was trying my BEST to get somewhere in life but even if the world around me was against me, I knew in my heart that God would provide a way.

THE LORD SHALL RENEW THEIR STRENGTH

I knew deep down that I had to be strong for my mom, sister and my younger brother. I may have fallen down, but it was time for me to get back up. It was time for me to move forward in faith again.

A year later, we received a letter for myself and my brother from the American Embassy with a date for a new interview. I couldn't wait to call my dad and let him know that there was finally a light at the end of the tunnel. HOPE had been restored!

I told him he did not have to come because he had spent so much money on my siblings. Still he pinched and saved so he could come over and take us to the American Embassy in Islamabad, the capital of Pakistan. We were ready, and with hopeful hearts we headed off to get our Visas.

ACTION STEP: *PREPARE*

I AM RELAXED EVEN THOUGH I MAY BE REJECTED.

List some of the ways you are preparing to overcome the obstacles in your life.

_____

_____

_____

_____

_____

_____

_____

_____

_____

_____

Rejection is emotionally difficult to manage. The best way to prepare is to know that God's Will, will be done in the end. Be faithful and do your best.
He will do the rest.

5

Believe in Miracles

For we walk by faith, not by sight

2 CORINTHIANS 5:7

I keep saying that Pakistan was corrupt, but you can't possibly understand unless you were raised there poor and struggling.

We had hoped our interview at the Embassy would be a quick "in and out" process. But when we arrived at 4:00 am the line was already two streets long. The rules were that you should wait in line with all of your papers together and until your number comes up. Then, at 4:00 pm the Embassy shuts their doors, and everyone is expected to come back every day until your number was called.

We stood in line for 10 days. We all were wearing the same clothes that we had arrived in. I had no idea it would take so long! I was ready to get out of there. I wanted to run far from this country and make a life somewhere meaningful.

The line was surrounded by security and cameras everywhere. I kept looking ahead and thinking, "There are still 50 people ahead of me so, we are going to have to come back again." Maybe we would get through on the 11th day or the 12th... but how could we know for sure?

We *wanted* to follow the rules and do everything properly; my father was insistent on that. We waited years for the letters to come, had all of the papers required and now, we were waiting in a line that was 10 days long.

We'd done everything right. We went through legal channels and payed huge sums of money that my family could not afford. We sacrificed everything for us to be there in that line so we could get that Visa and the wait was eating away at our faith. I knew I had to take matters into my own hands.

STRAIGHT IS THE GATE AND NARROW IS THE WAY

I was running out of time. There were only 10 minutes left until 4:00 pm came and they shut the doors for the day. So, I turned to my brother, grasped his hand and ran for our lives.

I ran straight through the security gates and said "I need to talk to somebody right now! I need to get somewhere!"

Shocked, the gentleman replied, "You can't just run in there, people are going to think you will harm them."

It didn't matter, I was desperate. I told him, "I need help! This is not right, we've been here for 11 days, wearing the same clothes just to get this visa. We have a letter saying we are approved, what is the hold up?"

He looked at me for a moment and then asked, "Who are you?" I showed him my papers. Then, he asked about my brother.

The floodgates opened. I told him the WHOLE story. I told him how we tried this a year ago, were rejected and that this time I was not going to let ANYTHING get in the way. I said, "I'm ready for my interview. I need that visa stamp on this paper…. please help us!"

I thank God every day that the man listened to what I said and went into the building to find the lady in charge. It was the same woman who interviewed me the year before. She came to the window and asked what was going on.

I try to explain to her in my broken English that I had been waiting for 11 days just to get this letter to her so that I can receive my Visa stamp. "We have been here and done everything the right way using all of the right channels. What is taking so long?" I asked

She looked at me and said "Oh. I remember you," and proceeded to ask me all of the normal interview questions.

I tell her that YES, I am going to college. YES, I will be working. YES, I will support my brother as he goes to school. "We just want to live our lives and have a happily ever after." I urged.

She began to look around the office for my folder to process my visa. She looked absolutely EVERYWHERE and could not find it. Meanwhile, I stood behind the window peering at every surface in the office trying frantically to help her from where I was. It was just *gone.*

Suddenly, I spotted a file that had slid under the edge of the office carpet, so I pointed to her saying "Look! What is that!" Sure enough, her assistant verified it was my file shoved under the carpet.

I don't know if it was an accident or malicious intent that landed my folder under that rug, but I am 100% sure that God showed it to me.

The woman opened our files and granted us the visa. Shaking my hand, she said "Thank you for what you did today. If you hadn't, you would be still waiting."

Shaking and relieved, I grasped my brothers' hand and walked back out the gates to meet my father. He was SO terrified that I had broken the rules and skipped the line.

My father had been pacing and shouting "Oh that's my daughter, she does these things…. she is not my daughter anymore!" He was cussing like crazy and when we finally stood before him, he asks, "Are you going to jail this time?"

So, I pulled out my paper and said, "Look dad, they gave us the Visa! We are going to America!" And just like that, I was a hero. "This is my daughter! Look what she did!" my father exclaimed. At that moment I decided that I was never going to sit back and let people walk all over me.

My father, brother and I rushed home to show my mom our Visas and buy our tickets to America. We were so excited.

A TIME TO GET AND A TIME TO LOSE

I was finally going to America. I felt it was my responsibility to take care of my younger brother because our mother would be staying behind with our older sister. The visa process was tricky, we had seen that. So, as we were walking to the airport, I kept looking back at my sister and my mother wondering if I would ever see their face again. Part of my heart was sad to leave even though I was excited.

The whole flight over we were thinking about how much our lives have changed. So much was now unknown. We had no idea what America was like and we hadn't lived with our father in many years. Honestly, we were worried that our father would not know what to do with us.

When we landed in Houston, Texas we were surprised to learn my brother and sister were not living with our dad as we had thought! They had moved to Virginia because he didn't want them to continue their education.

Another surprise was our dad decided to marry an American lady named Pat. She was sweet and treated my brother and I well. She helped me begin looking for colleges and get my brother enrolled in high school. Before we could start however, we had to take an English as a second language course.

My dad decided that I already had too much college and wanted me to go straight to work. My father insisted I pay him back for what he spent getting me and my brother to the US.

I agreed to work, as long as my brother could continue with high school. Due to a confusion with his education and his birthdate, he got his GED instead.

So, my brother and I decided to head to the nearest mall and apply at the stores inside. We thought about working in a Hallmark store (how hard could stacking cards be) or maybe an ice cream shop. We spent all day trying to talk our way into a job, thinking it would be easy. *It wasn't.*

Finally, a woman in the hallmark store asked me how long we had been in the United States. When I told her four weeks, she laughed and said, "You probably need another two or three years before you can get a job. Are you legal yet?"

Honestly, I didn't know what she was talking about. I thought the only way to get to America was the long and legal way I had experienced. I pretended not to be confused and told her, "I have a green card and in five years, I'll have my citizenship." I was proud of my green card and all the waiting I had done to get there!

She took pity on me and explained herself "I am asking because you need a credit history. You will need a driver's license, an address and previous work experience when you apply for a job."

"But I have to start somewhere! Who's going to give me a chance?" I wondered aloud.

IN ALL LABOR THERE IS PROFIT

My first job was working in my father's friends Laundry mat. They were a really nice Indian family and they had me working 40 hours each week. The whole time I was working, I was thinking "I went to college...I shouldn't be doing THIS. I should be going to school and continuing my education in America."

On my first paycheck there was a mistake. Apparently, I didn't input my hours right and they didn't want to pay me. We ended up having a huge argument and my step-mom said "Okay, we are not having you work there anymore. We will go someplace else." She immediately had me quit working there.

My next job experience was working at Jack-in-the-box in Houston as a cashier. On my first day a customer ordered a Dr. Pepper, and I got very confused. "Why would you order a doctor at a fast food place?" It took me some time to get used to American slang and new ideas such as soda.

My brother worked with me at Jack in the box as well. I'd like to be able to say we loved our new lives, but we were unhappy. This was not the life that we dreamed about when we stood in line for those visa papers. There just had to be more.

Then my sister called and made us an offer that was too hard to pass up. "Come to Virginia with us. I will buy both of your tickets. You can go to school if you want or keep working. Dad doesn't understand how important this is to us and how hard mom fought for us to be equally educated."

She was right.

All my father cared about was that we work and give him money. I WANTED to work. I WANTED to pay him back, but I wanted to do it in a way that wasn't a dead end. I wanted a degree in my hand and a career to call my own, not just a job. I had big plans for the lives my brother and I would build.

We knew we had to take this opportunity, so after talking with my dad and him admitting how painful it was for us to leave him, my brother and I flew to Christiansburg to be with my other siblings. As soon as we got there, we started looking around for a college that my brother could attend.

I decided to continue with accounting and started looking around at colleges. I had already done three years of college in Pakistan and I knew that language was not an issue for accounting. But unfortunately, in America it is not EASY to go to college.

You see, in Pakistan college is part of the government. The fee is once a year and the amount is minimal because in Pakistan college is required. In America you have to pay a full years fees up front and the cost is substantial.

After visiting the community college and showing them my transcripts, I learned that after three full years of college in Pakistan, only 17 credits were transferable. Basically, I had to start all over again.

I decided to work and save money for my college education and began working 35 hours a week as a cashier at Wade's supermarket making $4.05 an hour. I also started to learn better English at the community college on my time off. I made a good friend named Mary. She was also a cashier at Wades, and she had already been there for 20 years when I started.

She was a hero at work. She taught me how to scan and how to talk to our customers. Mary was one of the nicest people that I have ever met. She even used to leave me candies or sweets sometimes.

This was a hectic time of our lives. My four siblings and I were sharing a small apartment. All of us were working to keep a roof over our heads, food on the table and earn an education that could help in the long run. It was then that I realized that I would have to work every single day in order to afford living in America.

Healthcare was something else that came as a surprise to us. The Pakistan drivers licenses that my mother fought so adamantly for were no good in our new country, so my brother and I headed down to the DMV to get a proper license.

It was while I was squinting into the eye examiners face and asking why he was testing me in Japanese that I realized that I needed glasses. In Pakistan, glasses are shameful and if you wear them, you are considered ugly. Why couldn't I just catch a break?

I left the DMV so sad that my eyesight was weak. I took it as a personal insult to my character, but I also knew that to succeed in our new country I needed this license. For that, I needed glasses. So, I began trying to find some place to help me get them without health insurance.

Back home in Pakistan, everyone has health insurance automatically. In my mind, a full work week would pay for an eye exam and glasses.

At work the next day, my new friend Kathy suggest a few local optical centers. I picked a quaint little place and went in to speak with a lady. I showed her how much I make a week and I asked if I could pay off the glasses in four weekly installments. I believe an angel was watching out for me that day.

The nice lady wrote an agreement and we both signed it. That is how I got my very first pair of glasses. Three months later, I went into DMV nervous but determined and came out with my driver's license. Finally, it seemed like things were falling into place.

After three months at my job, I had established a regular work routine and knew that it was time for me to buy a car. My friend took me to one of those "Good credit, bad credit, no credit" dealerships and I found a 1988 Volkswagen Jetta that I liked.

I called my dad and asked him if he would co-sign the car with me and he said "No. You want to be on your own…go be on your own. I do not approve. I don't want you to buy a car because you are too young."

The guy ran my credit, saw that I had none and offered me credit anyway with a 32% interest loan. I was not happy. I told him I would buy the car because I needed it, but knew he was taking advantage of me.

I signed the deal and left with my new car, happy that I would be able to drive my siblings around to work and school. I was so proud of what I had accomplished so far.

Two months later, I found out that my older sister came from Pakistan and she was with my father. She too, didn't want to live with him and his wife. So, she came to Virginia to be with all of us.

Finally, all five of us siblings were together, living in a small apartment going to work and school every day and trying our very best to build successful lives.

Slowly, we started building those lives separately. My older brother joined the coast guard and my sister moved in with one of her friends. Since I was the one with a car and insurance, I continued taking my other sister and brother back and forth to work and school.

No, our lives weren't the dream we had envisioned before coming to America. But then does anything really ever live up to your childhood expectations? We were living legally and freely in a place that would allow us to create whatever live we were willing to work for.

I can't count the number of times it would have been easier to give up. I can't begin to tell you the number of tears that were shed in prayer and in frustration because everything around me screamed it was hopeless to dream.

Looking back, my heart aches for the people who settled, for the ones who believed the lie that they weren't capable of more. I thank God for the strong conviction I had to never give up.

And while it would take many more years of hard work for me to eventually create the life, I knew I was destined to live, I was comforted knowing that I was finally on the right path.

ACTION STEP: *BELIEVE*

I RELY ON FAITH TO PURSUE MY DREAMS
WHEN OTHERS WOULD HAVE GIVEN UP.

List some of the goals or dreams you have that seem
just out of your reach.

_____

_____

_____

_____

_____

_____

_____

_____

_____

_____

Now, pray for God to help give you a faithful spirit.
While you may feel pain from time to time, He will
provide for you according to His will. Have faith!

6

Semper Fortis

Be of good courage,
and he shall strengthen your heart,
all ye that hope in the LORD.

PSALM 31:24

Eventually, my sister started working at a local daycare and as it happened it was down the street from a Navy recruiters office. I noticed a man would stand out front in a nice uniform and talk to people that would pass by. I often found myself wondering if I should talk to him about joining the military.

I was working part time, in a dead-end job with low pay. I was struggling financially, and I had no benefits. I knew I didn't want to do that for the rest of my life and wondered if the Navy was the answer.

I kept my thoughts to myself of course, because I knew that my family would disapprove. But still, after a few days of it weighing heavy on my heart I decided to sneak down to that office and talk to that nice man.

He told me that the first step to serving was to take an ASVAB test. I had to receive a certain score in order to discuss the next step in the process. So, I took it and received a high score, so we discussed enlistment options.

The recruiter recommended a four-year enlistment to start and I agreed. I signed up, was sworn in and I went home to try and figure out how I was going to break the news to my family. I went home and only told my younger brother, because he always accepted everything about me without judgement.

TRUST IN THE LORD WITH ALL YOUR HEART

In case you haven't picked up on it yet, I was very naïve. I was only 18 years old and alone in a strange country with no parents to guide me. I had no idea what I was getting myself into, but I knew in my core this was what I was meant to do. So, I just went back to work and on with my day to day activities, with this secret hanging over my head.

My friend Mary was one of the very first people I told I was joining the service. "I don't know why I did it, but my heart told me to go for it!" I explained to her. She supported me fully saying, "Go for it!" I remember when I was younger, and mentioned I wanted to join the arms in Pakistan my family told me absolutely not!

Her encouragement was what I needed to hear. Knowing one person had my back was enough to get up the nerve to tell my manager. He quite literally dropped everything that he was holding to the ground. "Are you THINKING about joining or have you ALREADY joined?" he asked

"I already did." I answered proudly.

He proceeded to tell me horror stories and urge me to call them back and pull out of my agreement. "Look, you are too young and new to this country. You are just learning this world, why in the world would you just join the military. This is not right!"

A boy I had been sort of seeing at the time who had recently left the army and was studying to become a pastor was even dismayed. He put on the movie Titanic and told me "This is what is going to happen to any ship you go to!"

One of my friends told me "You can't take anything serious in there, as soon as you get off that bus people are going to start screaming at you. Just let it go in one ear and out the other."

Only a handful of friends understood my need to join the military and have the means to pay for my education. I wanted to show my appreciation to this beautiful country who saved me from my corrupt home. I wanted to stand on my OWN two independent feet and just like my mother wanted, I would take care of MYSELF.

So, after telling everyone around me, I knew it was time to tell my dad. I knew he would be furious, and I was scared. Growing up, we were raised to listen to our parents no matter what. One of the most important rules was NO arguing with parents.

When I told him he said "What? What is this? Do you just want a car? I will buy you a car, I will get you whatever you want just don't join the military. Don't leave."

BE STEADFAST AND UNMOVING

I was so angry. I have always been strong willed but am especially so when people tell me I *can't* do something. If someone tells me I will fail at something that makes me want to do it even more. So, I called my recruiter and said "I want to push up my date, the very next opening that comes up I want in." It was naïve of me.

I was sent to Richmond Virginia for medical and mental testing before I shipped out. When they checked my heart, they discovered I have a murmur and told me that it might prevent me from joining the Navy. I went back to my recruiter's office upset that I might be rejected. I was ashamed at the thought of telling my family that I couldn't join because I KNEW that they would laugh and tease me.

My recruiter decided to take me to another doctor's office. The doctor asked me to tell him what happened. I told him that I was so anxious the morning of the tests that I drank four cups of coffee. As a result, the doctor noted in my chart that the coffee made my heartbeat too fast and that I was medically fit to serve. Just like that, I was back on track to join and given a new date to ship out.

I was supposed to start bootcamp in July, but in March my recruiter called me up and said there was an opening for Memorial Day weekend. I accepted the new date.

When the time came for me to get on the bus, my younger brother told me that he wanted to join the Navy too. I told him, "Let me try it first, and I will let you know if you should join." I said goodbye and headed off for the next phase of my life: The United States military.

I laugh now thinking back at how unprepared I was. For example, I thought my friends warning about people yelling at me in the service was a joke. If only I had taken them seriously!

I was also deadly afraid of water, I know that sounds crazy since I joined the Navy, right? But my recruiter assured me that the good people in bootcamp would teach me how to swim and that I did not need to worry about it.

See, as a child, my parents did not let us go near any bodies of water because it would kill us. So, naturally my siblings and I grew up with a fear of swimming or drowning and there I was on a bus to join the Navy and I had no idea what I was doing.

As soon as we arrived at camp, an RDC (Recruiter Division Commander) started screaming and cussing until his face turned red and the veins popped out on his neck. We weren't even supposed to look at the RDC, because if you do, you'd have to drop and do pushups.

My natural personality is a happy one. I like to smile, and love to make others smile, too. As you can imagine within about five seconds, my personality had me on the ground doing pushups for trying to be nice. I had to drop five different times for pushups from the bus to the terminal. The whole time I was thinking, "What did I do to myself?"

I went into shock. What had I done? This is not a place I wanted to be. What was that 'F' word the Petty Officers keep using? I'm not allowed to smile. I can't seem to follow directions. In my panic, I thought that if this was the Navy, then I changed my mind about wanting to be a part of the military!

In my moment of despair, the sun shines on my face and I feel peace. I know I'll be fine. I can do this. God would see me through. And he did, though it didn't mean things would be easy.

There were 80 girls in our division and we quickly learned that we were expected to work as a unit, because if one person messes up, we all got punished.

In the midst of all the chaos that we were allowed a 3-minute family phone call. You were only allowed to say, "I'm good, I made it safe and I will talk to you in 8 weeks." I chose to call my younger brother because my dad told me I was dead to him for my choice. The rest of the family except my brother, followed is lead.

When my brother was on the phone and I told him, I was okay and for him to go to college, not join the military. I had never experienced anything like it and wanted to prevent my brother from going through it as well. Basically, they told us when to eat, when to pee and when to breathe. Every detail of our life was planned out for us.

It was hard for me to understand a lot of what people were saying around me at times. I didn't understand the curse words and the slang terms that everybody around me used. In the beginning I had no idea what was going on most of the time.

But I did make some friends that would help me, and we are still in touch to this day. One of them would even share her family letters with me because I had only two friends from Wades writing me and none of my family.

The first eight weeks, they make it as hard as possible. I stopped smiling. I stopped talking and become a shadow of my former self because I needed to survive. I couldn't help but think how I came to the United States only seven months ago.

I had to work twice as hard to learn everything compared to my teammates who had been born here. I was in a whole new world, eating brand new foods and learning how to keep to a strict time schedule. It was culture shock.

And at night, when I would lay in my cot asking myself if I did the right thing, again I'd feel that sense of peace. The fear, the doubt, the insecurity was all part of the process. I was going to get through it.

Throughout bootcamp, there are several different tests sailors are required to pass before graduating and moving on to A school. A school is where you would continue with training specific to the position you would hold in the fleet.

There was a mental exam, running, swimming and everyone had to do one week in the Galley. I thanked God every morning for the ladies who befriended me and helped me through that difficult part of my life. In fact, my friend Melissa stood up for me SO much that she would get in trouble and have to do pushups just to get her point across.

She would tell people to stop yelling at me and to speak to me calmly so that I could understand what was asked of me. She helped lift my spirits and I am thankful for her to this day.

The whole time I was at camp, I was waiting for them to send me off to learn how to swim because my recruiter told me they would teach. There were 80 of us in my team and we all had to pass our swimming test within a certain amount time.

As my turn got closer, I realized no one had approached me about my ability to swim and I started getting sick to my stomach. Swimming was my greatest fear in life, so I kept walking to the back of the line.

Finally, I raised my hand to tell them that I was ready to be sent off to a swimming class. They looked at me and announced that the people who didn't know how to swim were to make a line. My "lesson" was really only 30 minutes to face my biggest fear and learn how to swim. Then, I had another 30 minutes to jump off of the 20-foot-high diving board and swim a whole lap.

And I did it. I overcame the biggest fear in my life because I refused to fail. That challenge gave me confidence to tackle anything that I was fearful of.

How many times in life do we avoid taking a step or making a decision because we are terrified of the process? How many times do we focus more on our fear than the outcome of conquering it? If there is anything in this book that sticks with you, I want it to be this: DO IT SCARED.

Whatever IT is, do it anyway. Do it scared. Do it imperfectly. Do it purposefully and in spite of anyone else's objections. The only thing worse than not doing it, is wondering if you were the only thing standing in the way of your dreams.

Every week our team was getting smaller and smaller. Girls kept dropping out or getting sick. Our division started with 80 women and at the end we had shrunken down to only 45.

During my mental exam they realized that English was my second language and postponed my graduation by two weeks. I had to join another division and told to learn English and all of the military terms that were required within that two-week period. Unfortunately, I got sick and they added on two additional weeks. My Bootcamp ended up being 12 weeks instead of eight.

ENTERTAINING ANGELS UNAWARE

As graduation got closer, all of the girls became excited to see their families. While I was happy for my new friends, I was incredibly sad for myself because I knew that no one would be watching me pass this incredible challenge.

My friend Amber noticed that I had nobody and asked me if I wanted to join her and her family for the two days leave following graduation. Her mom and her sister were flying out and excited to meet me. I accepted and it moved me that these incredibly sweet, giving people were looking out for me.

During those two days, Ambers family encouraged me and told me "You are doing the right thing. It will work out. This was only the beginning for me." It felt good to have people cheering me on instead of making me doubt myself.

For two days, we bummed around Chicago, went to the mall and tried all kinds of different foods at restaurants. I had the best time of my life and it made me so thankful that God had placed those angels in my life.

The tiniest acts of kindness can make the biggest impact in a person's life. I know it did mine and I'm sure someone has left an impression in yours. It's so important that we treat people around us with kindness and respect.

After bootcamp I wasn't sure what field I wanted to go in so, I went undesignated to see what was available. For me, it was important that I find out more about my job options before signing up for it. I had learned that lesson the hard way through my enlistment.

In A school there were a lot more freedoms than bootcamp. We were scheduled for school from 9-5 and could come and go as we wanted. A lot of my friends partied and drank. While many of my friends took on the "we can do anything we want now" attitude, I kept my mind on the bigger picture. I did enjoy hanging out with friends on my time off but made sure to keep my focus on school and away from distractions like boys.

After A school I got two weeks leave to visit family before being stationed. I drove to Christiansburg and hung out with my brother. I visited my recruiter too. My parents and my sisters were still not talking with me because of the choice I made to join the military.

I did go and visit that boy I had been seeing, but he was not happy to see me. He thought that I joined the navy so I could find another man. I knew better and strengthened my resolve to keep my focus on my career.

I ended up getting stationed at Virginia Beach, ready to take on the next chapter of my life. As I look back now, sometimes I wonder how I survived this world with absolutely no support from my family.

The answer is God. He was constantly putting me in exactly the right place and surrounding me with people that I needed exactly when I needed them the most.

ACTION PLAN: *LET GO*

I CAN DRAW MY STRENGTH FROM GOD

List some of the things that you are struggling with or are overwhelmed by.

_____

_____

_____

_____

_____

_____

_____

_____

_____

_____

_____

_____

_____

Now, pray for guidance and turn them over to God.
Through Him, all things are possible.

PART THREE
FAITH

7

Marrying Mr. Right

Therefore, shall a man leave his father and his mother, and shall cleave unto his wife: and they shall be one flesh.

GENESIS 2:24

I can't express to you how important staying connected to your "why" is in terms of reaching your goals (no matter what those goals are). Whether it's to lose weight, land your dream job, start a business, start a family or even make an impact on others, you have to continuously keep your motivators in the forefront of everything you do.

I'd like to be able to say that once I got to my new station, things turned around. The truth is actually the opposite. I certainly didn't expect serving in the military to be easy. However, I constantly needed to remind myself why I was there and that it was only temporary.

If I'm being honest, in the beginning it was sort of dark and depressing. It was incredibly hard to make friends. There was so much I didn't understand about American culture. It made it really lonely at times. I just needed to make it through my term then I could go off to finish my college degree and build the dream life I'd been working toward for so many years. That meant I had to keep my head down, do my work and try to avoid distractions like boys.

Honestly, that wasn't as hard as you may think. I remember meeting a man from Pakistan at one point early on. I was blown away! I journey to this country, joined the Navy and just happened to meet this man who speaks the same language and is from the same country as I was. At first, I thought "WOW this is amazing; I have met my soulmate!"

Then he opened his mouth and spoke with the same prejudices that my family did. He said, "If I had a sister and she joined the Navy, it would kill my parents." That was all it took. Any respect that I had for him disappeared. "I'm not your sister." I replied, feeling my strength rear up and show its beautiful head. "This is what I want to do, and this is why I am here!" I insisted, stomping my foot for emphasis.

I knew that he wasn't a 'BAD' person. He just had the same mentality that people back home had. He believed girls shouldn't join the military because it was a man's world. I let his words slide off of my shoulders, like water off a duck's back. He was raised to believe things were supposed to be a certain way. He didn't have my mom in his ear telling him that girls are just as important as boys and capable of doing everything they desire.

FLEEING FROM SEXUAL IMMORALITY

In spite of our differences, I still befriended him and hung out with him when I got the chance. But his words NEVER left my mind; I never forgot where he stood with his beliefs. In the military, you have to make friends where you can. I was always really uncomfortable with all of the men cussing, speaking rudely to people or making sexual jokes. It was unprofessional and disrespectful.

I kept as far away from those guys as I could manage because there was NO way that I was going to let them talk to ME that way. We still had to take orders from our superiors without question of how they spoke to us, and that was always hard for me. I just wanted to work and earn my own way. But to blindly follow others...that was hard.

Once again, I felt myself sliding into depression much like back home, wondering why I had made the choices that led me to join the Navy. Any thoughts I had about running away was squashed by the thought of my family saying, "I told you so!" I am stubborn, I know my flaws and in this I was unwavering. I wanted to prove to my family and everyone who had disowned me, that I was able to succeed at this.

Everyone has stories of WHY they joined the military, for me it was to stand on my own two feet and be successful. Each story is unique. But if you asked any man at the time of my service, they would tell you that women only join the Navy to party or have sex. This made me SO angry and I felt my personality began to change as a result of those feelings.

I was getting used to hearing nothing but rude things from the men around me. They either wanted to party with me or get in my pants. I had no patience for that craziness, and I was grumpy to everyone around me. I would snap at people who tried to start conversations with me. I had become one of those "disgruntled' people who would try to put people in their place when they spoke to me.

Then one day a senior airman in the line shack I was working says to me "Do you know why girls are always mean?" I answered, "Because they can be, so you should stay away from nice girls." He seemed amused and insisted that all he wanted to do was say good morning and be friendly. Obviously, I didn't believe him with everything I had been exposed to. But as irony would have it, he would later become my husband.

That wasn't the only run in I had with that airman. As the days passed, I began to realize that his personality was just like mine USED to be. He was a happy person who enjoyed living his life. I felt so comfortable talking with him because he was so respectful compared the other men who were stationed with me. I could feel my temperament slowly start to relax.

After a few months of hanging out, Curtis and I realized that we liked each other far MORE than just friends. The problem was that he was a shipmate in the same workshop and my service contract forbade dating coworkers in the same shop. It made things very interesting. We had to keep our dating on the downlow.

Curtis liked to go on short road trips. It was on one of these trips that we decided it was time to visit my dad. I was so nervous on the four-hour drive to Christiansburg. I just knew my dad wouldn't like Curtis.

First, they didn't want me to join the military and I did it anyway. To add insult to injury, I was dating an American white boy. I just knew my parents would disapprove. I tried to prepare Curtis for the things he was about to hear. "Don't take anything serious, I'm sure they are going to say hurtful things, but we have to make light of it." I warned.

When we finally made it to my dad's, we acted casual and talked about the military. My dad explained his work and talked about how he worked for the Saudi airline. Everything was going well, until my dad looked at me and asked, "Are you going to marry this boy?"

I was so embarrassed. I did not want to talk about that in front of Curtis because I knew my dad would talk about his silly ideas for me. I said "No, he just wanted to meet you and make up for the time that you came out to see me when I was working." My dad accepted my answer, and we actually had a lot of fun on our visit. We went hiking, hung out and enjoyed each other's company. We even took dad out for a nice dinner and showed him the sights.

My dad decided he could trust me again and I was so happy. I really enjoyed being with him without the cloud of disapproval and shame hanging over me. This is also when my dad told me he hadn't been feeling well lately. He insisted he didn't want to talk about it. At the time, I thought that it was his way to get me to tell him that I accept his unspoken apology. "Dad, you don't have to say you're sick to get me to accept you. I love you and everything is going to be okay." He immediately changed the subject and we continued to enjoy our brief truce together.

THOU SHALT NOT VEX A STRANGER

After meeting my dad, Curtis wanted me to go to meet his parents. I was, of course, worried. My parents had decided that I was going to do what I want, and they had to accept it or live without me. But I wasn't sure how Curtis's family would take to me. But I guess that is how everyone feels when they go off to meet their boyfriend's parents.

When I met Curtis's mom and brothers for the first time, I could tell that I was a shock to them. They definitely didn't think that I had good intentions for him. Back then being from a middle east country made people leery and nervous. They asked me point blank if I was dating Curtis so that I could become a legal citizen. I was stunned. Obviously, I were here legally I couldn't have joined the service. They were harsh and it was uncomfortable, but we accepted it was just something we BOTH were going to have to deal with.

I'd like to say that gone are the days of racism and prejudice, but that's just not the way the world works. I remember Curtis's mom asking me weird questions like "How do you like having electricity?" or "Have you ever seen a car before?" I was astounded that they thought these things about my home country. I tried to understand. Curtis told me that they had never traveled anywhere. They were merely uneducated. I assured them that we had electricity and that we had our own car in Pakistan. We were young were determined to prove ourselves to them.

After meeting each other's families, it was time for us to be deployed. Curtis had joined the Navy two years before I did, and he was up for reenlistment. It was so hard sneaking around together and acting casual in front of others, and we couldn't move forward in our relationship if we had to keep it quiet. So, he decided to be discharged, let me finish out my term and then reenlist when I was done.

I had the hardest time during my deployment. To be honest I hate labor work. We were lugging chains everywhere, fueling the jets, parking them, changing the oil and chaining them to the flight deck. I had a supervisor who, if I looked tired or asked to use the restroom would tell me "You never should have joined the military. You want to act like you are equal to a man then be equal. Do the work."

At that time, I was working anywhere between 12-18-hour shifts and I was so scared to ask to use the bathroom, I stopped drinking water and became so dehydrated that I made myself sick.

THE VALLEY OF THE SHADOW OF DEATH

While still out to sea, I got an email from my brother telling me that our dad was not doing well. He felt dad was not going to live much longer. I was in shock! I knew that my brother would not reach out to me, unless the situation with our father was dire.

So, I immediately sought out my chaplain who instructed me to "Go to sleep. I will pray for you." I tried to explain to him how serious it was, and he insisted that sleep would make things better.

Frantic, I went to one of my officers with the situation and he was shocked at the chaplain's advice. He assured me that they would get me to my father no matter what. The Red Cross helped to get me off the boat and onto a plane to see my dad.

When I found out that he was in a hospice center in Miami, I couldn't believe it. I had just seen him not that long ago and had no idea that he was so sick. On my flight I had convinced myself that I would arrive, and he would be perfectly fine. I just knew he would get up and move around like it was all just a bad dream.

But it wasn't a dream. I got off in Miami with my sea bag and uniform and rushed to his place only to find out that he didn't recognize me. He was too far gone. 11 hours later he passed away. It was heartbreaking. He didn't even look like himself when he passed. He was so skinny from the weight loss and gaunt from the sickness. As I stood over him, I thought "I'm only 20 years old, and I just lost my dad." He died of prostate cancer because he refused to be treated. How could he let this happen?

We buried him the next day and I got on a plane back to Virginia. I spent a few weeks recouping and trying to come to terms with the death of my father. The man who wasn't physically with us a lot as children, but who worked himself to the bone to provide us with the opportunity for a better life. I was in shock. I didn't even cry. I just couldn't believe that it had happened at all.

When my deployment was over, my siblings were all getting finished with college. They were all moving on and getting jobs. It finally felt like everything was working out like it should. Curtis was honorably discharged from the Navy and was trying to decide whether to go to college or become an AC technician.

I was focused on trying to finish my college degree. And, since Curtis was no longer my superior, we were finally free to get married!

THEY SHALL BE ONE FLESH

In Pakistan, weddings are SUPER traditional and 'showy'. You deck yourself out with gold and jewels and the festivities typically last for seven days. I knew I did not want to have a wedding like that. I was more than happy to go into a court and get married over a desk, but Curtis wanted a traditional wedding and he thought it would be good for me to have that experience.

Luckily, Curtis's grandmother took me under her wing and taught me everything about weddings in America. She helped me look for something old, new, borrowed and blue and schooled me on the garter ceremony. She helped me order a wedding cake (which was new to me) and took care of my fancy dress. She was such a blessing to have at my side on one of the most important days of my life. We got married at the chapel on base and the entire family enjoyed the day together.

Nine months after our wedding, I was close to being discharged from the Navy and excited at the idea of starting a family. Even if we didn't have children right away, I could work and FINALLY live the happy life that I had been dreaming of. Unfortunately, 9/11 happened and the military put a hold on my discharge.

All of a sudden, my plans for my life were put on hold. The military ordered me to stay active because they might need me or my language skills on future missions. Even though my four years were up, everyone I spoke too gave me the run around and refused to let me leave. It was frustrating.

I served my new country and worked hard for four years. Now, I wanted to build a family with my husband and create the life that I had dreamed of for many years. So, I wrote my local congressman and sought approval to be discharged from the Navy. At one point, a career counselor approached me. It was her job to get service men and women to extend their time in the military.

She was rude and racist, and she made me furious. She tried to bully me into reenlisting. She told me, "You know, nobody will hire you because of your accent. You are from a different country and nobody can even understand the things you say. You are better off just reenlisting and staying with us.... We are the only place that will accept you."

I knew it was her job to try and talk me into staying, but the way that she was approaching me was incomprehensible. I responded, "I HAVE made up my mind, I did my time and served my country. Now, I am going to go to college like I always planned, and I will raise a family."

Being from another country and looking different had always been hard but being from another country that was scary. Living in a post 9/11 world didn't just impact me. Curtis was dealing with his own drama from people putting their '2-cents' into our relationship. His friends and family were telling him that he shouldn't be married to me "I bet she has a knife or a gun next to her bedside to kill you with. That explains why she is here." They told him, and "She is from THAT country, I don't know how you can even live with her."

As a result, Curtis and I had to develop something we call the "Switch". We trained ourselves to just stop listening when people spoke negatively and switch our attention to more positive things. It was the only way that we would get through BOTH of our families prejudices and insecurities with OUR relationship intact.

I ended up going above that rude ladies head. I talked to an Equal Opportunity Officer and explained what she had said to me. The woman ended up getting in trouble and I thankfully, ended up receiving a letter from my congressman with an approval for an honorable discharge from the Navy. We could finally get on with our lives.

Curtis told me once, early on that I was his completion. I didn't know what to say at the time. People didn't say those things in real life. It was like something out of a poetry book. Yet after everything we have endured and more than 20 years together, I know he is the man God intended for me.

ACTION STEP: *PATIENCE*

YOU ARE WORTH OF LOVE

List some of the blessings God has provided for you.

_____

_____

_____

_____

_____

_____

_____

_____

_____

_____

_____

Now, pray to God thanking Him for these and future blessings. You deserve to receive love in abundance from those around you, just as you do from God.

8

Joys of Motherhood

Train up a child in the way he should go:
and when he is old, he will not depart from it.

Proverbs 22:6

One thing we knew for sure about our married life was that Curtis and I did not want to waste money on renting a home; instead we wanted to buy one. We were so proud of our choice because it meant we would be the FIRST ones in both of our families to own a home. Of course, we both took heat from our families because we were 'too young' to buy a home and 'too young' for that much responsibility. But we turned on our "switches" and did it anyway.

Excited at the first step toward building our own family, moved into our new home. It was a great experience. We had friends over to visit and got a dog. We even decorated our home for our very first Christmas together. We spent so much time deciding what we wanted our future to look like.

FOR EVERYTHING THERE IS A SEASON

I decided to go back to college because it was paid for by the military, so we didn't have to worry about acquiring student debt. I also worked part time at a bank and loved my job. It felt as though all my dreams from childhood were slowly coming true.

But you know what they say about the best laid plans… While we were busy "living our best life", I became pregnant with our first son Clint. This was great news! We knew we wanted a family, there was just a hitch in the timing of it all. Obviously, I was going to need medical care for the pregnancy and unfortunately, Curtis had missed the sign up date for coverage.

So, we put our positive brains together to create a plan. We definitely did NOT want to go to our families for help because they never supported our relationship or our choices. The alternative was for Curtis to reenlist because the medical coverage would be amazing. While it had always been his intention to reenlist, the coming baby sped that timeline up. And of course, the military was happy to have him back in service.

The good news is we were going to be relocated to Maine near his father. The bad news was that we only had two weeks to move. Luckily, one of our friends was looking for a new home and they offered to pay off our loan and move in within two weeks! The Lord had provided for us during a scary and uncertain time.

We packed up our cars (and our dog) and hit the road to our new life. The only hiccup we had in our travels to Maine was my horrid and unrelenting morning sickness. Once we made it successfully, we stayed with some of Curtis's family until we could find a home of our own. We ended up buying a double wide in Maine that was 30 minutes from Curtis's work and our son Clint was born a couple of months after we settled in.

HER CHILDREN ARISE UP, AND CALL HER BLESSED

Motherhood is another era of my life that opened a whole new meaning of God's love for us. Just the thought of him depending on Curtis and I for his life until he is an adult was so emotional for me, that I cried holding his little hand the whole ride home from the hospital. I even remember listening to Phil Colin's song "You'll Be in My Heart" from Tarzan during the drive.

We decided it would be better for me to stay home with Clint so Curtis could focus on his career. While sad being so far away from my family, it was nice that I got to spend some time getting to know my father in-law. We became good friends even though our time together occasionally made me miss my own father.

However, I'd be lying if I said being a stay at home mom didn't take a toll on our marriage. I was taking care of our son alone and was always exhausted. I was also sad because although I loved my husband and child, it felt like my dreams were on hold. I was not furthering my education like I had always planned, and I had no career. On top of it all, Curtis would come home after a bad day and take it out on me. While it's normal to have fights and arguments in a marriage, I felt compelled to do more with my life.

Since money was tight, it appeared the solution to my worries was for me to find a job to help out. I tried all of the 'work from home' jobs that I saw advertised but got absolutely nowhere with them. Then, I saw a job advertised for a dog food company named Nutro.

They were hiring demonstrators to work four hours on Saturday and Sunday for $11.00 an hour. It was ideal! That would help us with gas money and extra things that we needed to make living more comfortable. Plus, I felt better about myself because I was contributing again.

Everything had finally started to feel more normal with managing the house, taking care of Clint and working part time when we found out that I was pregnant again. At the same time Curtis's father Craig became very sick with emphysema and heart issues, so I was taking him to and from appointments alongside everything else.

I became exhausted and depressed again and often needed to vent to Craig. I would say things like:

"Look at my life! I'm raising kids and staying home when all I wanted to do was go to college and get my degree!"

"I want to have a real job that can ease our financial struggles. What kind of life is this?"

"Do you even see me? I'm always running around with my son or gathering firewood and I'm pregnant again…what am I doing with my life besides staying home and taking care of you and our son?"

Bless his heart. He would always smile and say, "I DO see you Naseem, I see you going to those big meetings, and doing conferences." I would ask him, "How can you see me like that, past this snowstorm?" I felt like I was never, ever going to get there yet he was so sure I would see my hearts desires.

By that time, we'd been in Maine for three years and knew Curtis would be getting new orders soon. We were all so sad to be leaving, especially his dad. He couldn't accept the fact that we were leaving him. It made us all so sad. His dad had been my only friend and confidante during a lonely and lost time, and I would miss him so. Then, in July of 2006 he passed away. We were heartbroken. We were worried he had died of sadness from our departure and it made us feel even more guilty.

In August of 2006 our second son Carl was born, and we sold our home in Maine. We found out that Curtis made rank and planned to head back to Virginia and buy a small house. Once again, we packed up our cars and our kids and headed back to Virginia.

Unfortunately, every job I applied for was a rejection. At that time, being a military spouse made it very, VERY hard to find work because of the chance you would get called away. By then Clint was almost four years old and ready to go to preschool and I was more than ready to resume my education.

I eventually got a job working at a bank in the wire department and found and American public university online. I found myself working full time at the bank, with two small boys at home and pursuing my dream of a degree.

While I was happy working at the bank, I was still keeping my options open for better opportunities.

When I saw a job opening at one of the largest CPA firms in our area I applied right away. I always wanted to be an accountant knew I would regret not trying for the position.

I got called in for an interview but was told almost immediately that the job was offered to someone else because I wasn't the right candidate. Of course, rejection hurts, even if it's from a near stranger. So, I went on with my bank job, happy to have it.

Then, two months later I get a phone call from the CPA firm asking if I was still interested in the job I had applied for! It was more money than I was making at the bank and they wanted me to start the very next day. It was like a dream come true!

I began work as an accounts payable clerk at Goodman & Company and continued working on my degree when I wasn't at work. Everything was finally working out! My work was five minutes away from my house and my mom came and live with us, because Carl was only six months old and I didn't want to put him in daycare. We had a nice big four-bedroom house so she could have her own space. Things were looking up again.

When my company decided to move to Virginia Beach, Curtis and I decided to move there as well. We rented out our house and bought another house near my work, but my mom wouldn't be going with us. My brothers and sisters were all having babies and they needed her to help them out too. So, even though I hated the idea of putting Carl in daycare, we had no choice.

The funny thing about getting everything you've ever wanted is the feeling of guilt that often comes with it. As mothers, we tend to believe that our desire to have a successful career means either we are unsatisfied with being a parent or that our children will suffer in priority. We get so used to putting everyone else's needs first that the moment we shift our focus to something with personal gain, we feel selfish.

The truth is that parenting is the most rewarding, difficult experiences you can be blessed to have. It's scary, lonely and often thankless yet it is also so fulfilling. It teaches you what it means to love completely and unconditionally.

But even in all the wonder that is being a parent, we have to remember that God made each of us with a greater purpose in mind. He equipped each of us with unique talents and gifts that he intended for us to share with others. We are a "whole" person that needs to nurture and grow in our gifts to serve the Lord.

ACTION STEP: *FORGIVE*

GOD FORGIVES YOU. FORGIVE YOURSELF.

List some of the ways you feel you are selfish
when it comes to parenting.

_____

_____

_____

_____

_____

_____

_____

_____

_____

_____

_____

Now, pray for God to take them from your heart.
Remember, as a parent you're a whole person, too. It is
OK to say no to others and take time for yourself.
Show yourself grace.

9

You're Meant for More...
Build Your Dream

And be not conformed to this world: but be ye transformed by the renewing of your mind, that ye may prove what is that good, and acceptable, and perfect, will of God.

ROMANS 12:2

When you are a military spouse, you develop coping skills so that you can do it ALL. I had three full time jobs: taking care of our kids, taking care of the household and taking care of my work. I just had to tack on one more, finishing my education.

And I did.

In 2010 I finished my degree and had a great home life with the boys. Since I finally held my degree, I felt it was time to advance my career. So, when a job in management opened with my employer, I went to talk to my boss. I told her that I had been working there for three years, had a degree and would like to move up in the company.

While she allowed me to apply for the job, she ended up giving it to someone who had not worked there for two years and did not have any experience. Confused, I went to speak to her about it and he said "A degree is not needed for your job. You are fine without one here."

I just didn't understand her thought process. I wanted to work hard and move up in the company. How could they not value a formal degree from college? With a broken heart, I realized that I would never be successful at this company and started looking for a new job.

Eventually, I found a new job that I loved handling both bookkeeping and payroll clients for my employer. My career was on a roll and even though my boys were super high energy and exhausted me, I was so happy.

When spring vacation rolled around, I hit a bump in the road. Vacation meant the boys would be out of school and childcare would be closed. I had no help or support while Curtis was away, so I approached my boss and offered to work from home for those two weeks, but he denied my time off saying, "There is no flexibility. Find a babysitter and do the work you were hired for."

It reminded me so much of the being in the service. In the military, THEY come first no questions asked. But to ME, family came first. Since I had already served my time in the military, I was not about to let another person treat me like that again.

That was the last straw. I typed up my resignation and handed it in to my boss, happy to walk away from my job for the sake of my children and family. I didn't even tell my husband until after it was done. I simply made the decision and had no regrets because I believe that everything happens for a reason.

I stayed home for those two weeks and played with my boys, relaxing and enjoying the life we worked so hard for. When my husband called and I told him what I did he said, "That is fine, there is something wrong with the way they didn't even give you a chance. You always help anyone who needs it." And just like that, my husband lifted me back up on my feet.

After spring break was over, I spent several weeks searching for a new position more suited to my family and lifestyle. I took it one day at a time until I found an ad that looked promising. I eventually landed an office manager position of running an entire accounting department. It was a huge pay raise from what I was making before.

I was THRILLED! I reported to the CEO who was retired military. He was very kind and understanding of my family needs.

While I very much enjoyed my job, I still had this pull that there was something missing.

THY WILL BE DONE

You see, throughout all my experiences in life I would tell people, listen to that soft voice speaking words of encouragement in the back of your mind. The silent cheers when you overcome an obstacle or claim a victory. That voice is very powerful.

Knowing yourself well enough to trust in your convictions and have faith that God will provide a way for you. Those that refuse to get so caught up in their circumstances that they can't hear him speak to the bigger picture. They can live in abundance. I had so much to be thankful for, yet that voice told me not to settle.

I wasn't fulfilling God's purpose for my life yet. I was not being ungrateful; I was simply waiting for the Lord to tell me what he had planned next.

That voice told me to run into the Embassy or I'd never leave Pakistan.

That voice told me he would protect me while I served my new country.

That voice told me to relentlessly pursue my education.

And now, that same familiar trusting voice told me I didn't have to work for anyone else. I knew I had to listen to that voice to open to the next chapter of my life because the entrepreneurial seed had been planted in me years ago in passing conversation with friends and family. Even they knew skill was valuable enough to stand as its own business.

Of course, there were other motivators too. My oldest son was misdiagnosed as having subaortic membrane disorder requiring open heart surgery. The process of getting a second opinion on that diagnosis was so long and terrifying. Thankfully, my son was fine. However, it was confirmation that I was destined for more than a 9-5 job.

A "normal" job wouldn't have allowed me to be present for my son and fight for the care he needed. Building my own business was the only way I was going to be able to utilize the talents God gave me, provide an income and have the flexibility to be the mother my children deserve.

I knew that what I was doing for one client or one employer, I could do for various small companies. I knew it would save them from having to hire a full-time finance person and allow them to run their business with one less stressor. I knew I was capable of performing my duties from my home. After asking my sweet husband his opinion and getting his support, I decided to turn a dream into a reality.

THE LORD SHALL OPEN UNTO THEE HIS GOOD TREASURE

So, I looked at my finances to determine what I needed to accomplish with my income. To start, I wanted to help my husband pay for my monthly car payment and I needed to be able to keep up my QuickBooks certification.

My plan was to simply start networking with people and ask them if they needed help with business finances or payroll. I came up with a business name, printed cards, put up a website, paid my local and SCC fees, then got to work. And God rewarded my hard work.

My business began to grow. The first client I landed needed bookkeeping services for her nonprofit. Her fees were enough to cover my car payment. Confirmation number one. My second client was a renovation contractor and his fees were enough to pay our electricity bill. Confirmation number two.

I was actually working for myself and setting my own hours. I finally had the courage to start networking in business groups. It was then that I landed my third client - teaching her how to run her own bookkeeping. It was all real. My business continued to thrive and grow. Thank you, Jesus!

When I opened my business, I thought I had nothing to lose. I had quit a decent job, my son was sick, my husband was away with the military often leaving me alone with my sons and planned to do so for 20 years. Yet through it all, God was steadfast. He provided everything we needed in his timing.

Today, I have a full-fledged business where I'm paying myself a full-time salary. I even started a 401k just for my business. I can work on my own terms and take as much time off as I want to be with my family. I even get to work with people who I'm passionate about helping. I have so much joy in my life; it's almost as if all the things I went through were from a whole other lifetime.

What would have become of me if I had listened to the people who wanted to keep me small? Do you feel like you have been stumbling around in the dark, failing to live up to your potential? Do you feel there is some insurmountable obstacle preventing you from making changes in your life? If so, I beg you to turn it over to God in prayer.

Every time I faced horror, or disappointment or sadness, His love and grace were there to carry me until the smoke cleared enough that I could see His vision for my life. He will do the same for you, too.

ACTION STEP: *DREAM*

YOU ARE WONDERFULLY MADE

List some of the things you would love to accomplish in your life. What are the barriers?

_____

_____

_____

_____

_____

_____

_____

_____

_____

_____

Now, pray for God to give you clarity to see the path around those obstacles. Remember, it's ok to have goals and dreams! Your talents and gifts are often a blessing to others.

REFLECTION

*Delight thyself also in the Lord: and he shall
give thee the desires of thine heart.*

PSALM 37:4

Self-reflection not only functions as a humbling experience for showing God's graceful hand, but it's an incredibly powerful tool for personal and professional growth. It's almost as if you have your own personal time machine allowing you to weave throughout space and time.

When I was a young girl in Pakistan, I never once imagined I'd journey to America, join the military and build a successful business. Society told me I wasn't capable. But I prayed and studied, and I eventually leaped over the last obstacle preventing me from starting a better life.

When my family all but disowned me for joining the U.S military and the people around me tried to drown me with their prejudice, the Lord kept my head above water.

When I thought that I would never meet a man who would accept my passion and ambition as virtues and love me in spite of what others said, God gave me Curtis.

When I opened my business, I thought I had nothing to lose. I had quit a decent job, my son was sick, my husband was away with the military often leaving me alone with my sons and planned to do so for 20 years. Yet through it all, God was steadfast. He provided everything I needed in his timing.

Reflection allows us to lock onto any single, seemingly insignificant moment in your life and uncover the single thread that binds all of the events that follow it, as if stitching together the most delicate Thomas Kinkade tapestry. I call this the blessing point.

THE BLESSING POINT

All the roads we take lead to a blessing point; all the heartache and disappointment, as well as all the victories and blessings. It's also what we named our beautiful home (the view from which is pictured on the book cover). It represents everything we have done, and God has provided in our lives.

I'm so blessed to have this beautiful life and I want you to have one too. This book was not written because I wanted to tell my story. It was written because if I at any point would have listened to the world around me instead of putting my faith in God, I wouldn't be here today.

I desperately want you to know that no matter where you come from, how humble or foreign your beginnings or how much others try to prevent it, you CAN overcome it all to create the life of your dreams. I wanted this book to offer action steps you can use to navigate the journey.

Many people in your life won't get it. And that's ok. I do. God does. You are worthy and capable of the things you want. All you have to do is go get them.

Made in the USA
Columbia, SC
23 December 2019

85473684R00071